MUTED GREY

Dianna Young

MUTED GREY

Dianna Young

A Novella

Wildflower Press

ISBN: 978-0-9835332-0-7
LCCN: 2011934572

Wildflower Press
Publishing, Inc.
P.O. Box 3362
Rapid City, SD 57709

For my family

Two wrongs, it's been said
A right does not make
But alas, it's still human to try

Yet neither here nor there
These faded lines can I bear
Despite the log in my eye

Nay I'll stop right there
Lest you think that I judge
For I of all people can see

The error of my ways
Shall haunt all my days
Of such burdens I'll nary be free

~Achaia Ebere

PROLOGUE

Long legs extended gracefully as the muscles in her toned calves flexed with each stride. She clenched her fists, swinging her arms forward and back, urging her agile body onward, the bare soles of her feet gliding along the cool grit of the sandy beach. She approached an incredible white horse standing impatiently by the shoreline, stomping its hooves and sending sprays of sand flying about beneath him.

Skillfully, and without hesitation, her left hand firmly grasped the brilliant-white mane of the magnificent stallion. Throwing her right leg up and over, she hoisted herself onto the bare back of the steed. She kicked her heels into the animal's side as, quickly, she brought him to a full gallop, her lustrous black hair flowing regally in the breeze.

Racing onward, she approached a crowd assembled near the water's edge. Pulling fiercely at the reins, she brought the majestic beast abruptly to a halt at the shore where a group of women had gathered. They were of varying ages and ethnicities, all in flowing blue gowns.

One woman began sobbing softly; soon another began to cry. Eventually all were wailing inconsolably. Then, in unison, as if on cue, they turned and looked at her pleadingly, their desperate gazes piercing the depths of her soul. Ominous clouds reeled in the agitated sky above as the scene around her began to turn eerily gray.

Then the crystalline water, with its snow-white foam crashing upon the shore, turned blood-red, and the cries and sobs turned to shrill shrieks and piercing screams. The beautiful white horse upon which she rode turned coal black, its nostrils flaring as it thrashed violently. The stallion's wild eyes turned fiery as the animal reared, throwing her into the raging red sea, its waves like tentacles, pulling her down, deeper and deeper into the underbelly of the thick darkness in the foreboding abyss.

Dr. Marah Edom awoke on a beautiful Friday morning to her usual A.M. migraine which was exacerbated by the merciless bleating of her alarm. With brute force, she pummeled the snooze button on her clock. Then, with her eyes still shut, she opened the drawer to her night stand and felt around until she found a bottle of ibuprofen. Outside her window, beyond the barrier of closed blinds, occasional fluffs of white clouds were scattered about in the otherwise clear blue sky above. Birds sang melodiously as they perched on the low lying branches of the Sycamore tree outside. It was a perfectly glorious day to be alive. Yet, all Marah wished for was Saturday, darkness, and silence. If only she could sleep in. If only she could curl up in the cocoon of her covers and drown out the world around her. *If only.*

She'd had the dream again, that recurring nightmare which she could never quite put out of her mind. All the drugs in the world couldn't keep her from that dream which persisted in drowning out any chance of a good night's sleep. Lord knew she'd tried them all. Over the years, she'd come to rely on a series of mostly over the counter remedies to help knock her out, followed by others to wake her up, sandwiched between still others to help fight off the hangover effects of whichever remedy she was currently coming down from at the time.

She'd completed her under-grad, plus four years of med-school, followed by another four years of residencies. But none of her educational training had prepared her for the inane sense of dread she felt when faced with the task of getting up and going to work every day. She rolled out of bed with an audible groan and tossed three ibuprofen into her mouth, which she washed down with a nearly empty glass of Cabernet Sauvignon that remained on her night stand from the evening before.

Slowly, deliberately, she turned the blinds, revealing the unfortunate sunlight which threatened to send her migraine into the next zip code. Squinting through the glaring brightness, she worked her way toward the bathroom. As her eyes adjusted to the sunlight, Marah scarcely noticed the magnificent view outside, which at one time had made her heart soar.

Years earlier, on the day she first toured this house with her realtor, the view had taken her breath away. This, she had told herself, was what it was all about. All her hard work had finally paid off. This house, with its stunning architecture and impressive view, was her reward. The day she signed the papers to close on her beautiful Malibu beach home was the happiest day of her life.

She'd earned this. Yet, now that it was hers, she rarely had the time or energy to appreciate it. She lived in solitude with her cat, which demanded little more than a daily feeding and the occasional indulgence of a scratch behind the neck. Wrapped in a silk robe, Marah padded to the kitchen and opened a can of organic cat-food for her aptly named room-mate, 'Kitty.'

The invigorating scent of freshly brewed coffee lured her to the far end of the kitchen where her coffee maker, which brewed her first cup of java at precisely 6:30AM daily, sat faithfully awaiting her arrival. She passed the recycling bin on the way and tossed the empty can before reaching the opposite end of the kitchen, where she poured a cup of strong black coffee in an oversized terra-cotta mug. She hastily choked down the elixir which would relieve her fatigue while simultaneously sending her stomach into violent fits of rage.

Shuffling back toward the bedroom, Marah slid out of her robe before pulling on a freshly washed pair of shorts and a sleeveless cotton t-shirt. Then she slipped on a pair of gently worn running shoes which she quickly laced up. She stepped out the arcadia door, pulling it shut behind her, before propelling her body beyond the berm separating her home from the public beach.

Falling into a natural stride, she glided toward the compacted damp sand where the crashing waves made a hasty retreat into the ocean as streams of foam and seaweed trailed behind on the glistening shore. Supercharged by endorphins, she sprinted along the beach, enjoying the taste of the salty sea air. It was hard to top the way she felt when she ran. It was, in fact, the only time she ever felt truly alive.

An hour later, after Marah had showered and dressed for work, she drove along the Pacific Coast Highway in her red BMW convertible toward her office in Santa Monica. At precisely 7:45AM she pulled through a drive-in coffee shop where she was greeted by a young girl who looked up from her college textbook long enough to pass Marah's usual, a tall skinny latte with a triple shot of espresso, through the window. Marah had a standing order and an account with the shop, so there was no exchange of money, just a quick goodbye before she drove off. Soon after, Marah wheeled into the clinic parking lot and pushed a button on the console, setting the automatic closure of the convertible into motion. As the smooth humming sound of the top came to a stop she grabbed her Louis Vuitton purse and her coffee, then pushed the button on her key fob to activate the alarm.

"Show time," she said to no one but herself as she donned an award-winning smile and, after swiping her key-card, entered the back door to the private practice clinic which she had operated for the last five years.

CHAPTER ONE

Amaranth stretched lazily in the large four poster bed, her bright blonde curls cascading around her narrow shoulders, as she savored the warmth of Tad's hand on her thigh. She nuzzled up to his chest and spontaneously kissed him on his sun-tanned shoulder. He rolled toward her and offered one of those sleepy smiles that usually made her melt. But today, she thought willfully, was *not* going to be one of those days. Tad had always possessed some sort of power over her. She'd relinquished that power freely and realized this was entirely of her own doing. But, as she was well aware, she had a tendency to forget her own concerns at the expense of Tad's wishes. But, she resolved, today was a new day and from now on, things were going to be different. This, she determined, was ultimatum time. After much deliberation and serious consideration, she knew exactly what she would say. Her heart raced as she tried to form the words. Then, out of nowhere, as though she had not been rehearsing this in her head for days, the words gushed out without warning.

"I love you," she blurted, as if she were playing a game of charades and had been trying to beat the other opponents by saying it first. Then, as though her first declaration was not enough, "What do you think about getting married?" she asked as she grimaced awkwardly.

She wondered for a moment who had spoken. This was not part of the fully scripted, pre-meditated talk she'd been working and re-working in her mind for days. As she performed a mental rewind, she realized it was she who had uttered those fateful words. Amaranth groaned inwardly, realizing that for all her planning, she had more than likely just committed relationship suicide. She held her breath, waiting. Maybe he hadn't even heard her.

She studied Tad as he willed his tired eyes open, clearly struggling to bring his groggy mind into focus as he attempted to process what she'd just said.

"Are you serious?" he blundered. Then seeing the look on her face, "Oh, you *are* serious," he murmured, as he self-consciously looked away, nervously running his fingers through his sun-bleached hair. "Sorry, I just didn't think that was in the game plan for us. We were just taking things easy--weren't we?" he implored, his forehead wrinkled as he urged his foggy brain to transmit the words which his mouth now uttered.

"You know I love you," he said, not at all convincingly. "But," Tad spoke hesitantly, "I thought we weren't looking for that kind of commitment. I'm not sure I'll ever be ready for that," he said somewhat apologetically. "Now, come here," he beckoned in a deep, gravelly voice as he adeptly pulled her closer to him.

Tears pooled in Amaranth's eyes as she freed herself from Tad's grasp and out of his bed, willing herself to be liberated of him and any control he may have once had over her. She stretched a tank top over her head, pulled on a floral print skirt, then slid her feet into a pair of flip flops.

Without another word, she gruffly retrieved a large duffel bag from behind the closet door. It was the same bag she had used to cart her things back and forth between her condo and Tad's house over the past two and a half years. Then, angrily removing her clothes from his closet, without bothering to take them off the hangers, she began stuffing them into the bag.

Rounding the corner to the bathroom, she used one hand to slide her toiletries from the countertop into a heap on top of the overflowing bag. Then she gave the duffel a quick shake, forcing the contents to settle so she could make more room inside. Swinging the medicine cabinet door open, she searched inside for any remaining personal items. Eyeing her diaphragm case, she forcefully clutched it and, with a growl, gave it a heave toward the garbage can, missing her aim entirely.

She took one last look at the room as she mentally chided herself. What a fool she'd been to waste her time working with Tad to remodel this room the year before. She'd even helped him install the white porcelain tile which, she recalled acridly, had done wonders to brighten the room. What a joke, she thought. How had she ever managed to convince herself that she belonged here? She hastily collected the remainder of her scant belongings before storming down the long hallway toward the front door. She didn't look back; she didn't say another word. It was over. Not bothering to zip the duffel bag, she gave the front door a shove, letting the screen door crash as it slammed shut behind her.

"Fool!" she shouted, more at herself than anyone else, when she realized he wasn't coming after her.

Deep down, she'd always known that she and Tad had no prospects for a future together. Ultimately, what she had convinced herself was a relationship, had never been anything more than an extended fling in his eyes. Not once ever had he implied a yearning for anything more than the shallow and meaningless relationship they'd shared over the past years. But somehow Amaranth had chosen not to acknowledge that fact. She had wanted to believe he was capable of loving her and needing her back.

Now, in retrospect, Amaranth realized she'd been settling all along. With startling clarity, she was struck with the revelation that she could no longer accept this relationship for what it was, what it would always be. She'd rather be alone than in this relationship which had long since reached a dead end on the road to potential.

She was fairly certain her departure would not leave a hole in Tad's life; in fact, she knew with utter certainty that he'd move on in short order. He was probably contemplating her replacement at this very moment. For all she knew, he might already have a string of women on reserve for an occasion such as this, just waiting to warm her side of the bed. As her mind conjured images of Tad with her replacement, caustic bile rose from her stomach, introducing a foul taste to her mouth. As she grabbed her keys and cell phone from her purse, she dialed the number to her office.

"Tamara, this is Amaranth," she announced with more confidence than she felt. "I won't be in the office today. I've got something I need to take care of," she finished, as she pressed her forehead against the car door and took several shallow breaths before exhaling deeply.

Then, powering off her phone, she threw open the car door, tossed her duffel bag on the back seat, and climbed inside. She put the key in the ignition and started her car. Amaranth wasn't sure where she was going; she just knew she needed to clear her head. She didn't need to be anywhere until afternoon, so she put the car in gear and began driving without any real destination in mind. She soon found herself winding along the Pacific Coast Highway.

She drove until she came across a secluded patch of sand with a small gravel parking area nearby. She got out of the car and walked toward the tranquil shore where the waves seemed to beckon her. Kicking off her shoes, she meandered lazily until she arrived at the smooth wet sand of the shoreline where strands of seaweed clung to enormous chunks of sun-bleached driftwood. She found a dry patch of sand nearby where she sat, indulging herself, as the sun warmed her from above. She wriggled her toes deep beneath the gritty, translucent granules, down to the wet sand below, which clung to her sun-tanned feet.

Off in the distance, a little girl with a halo of white curls spun round and around, her arms outstretched as she basked in the glory of the early morning light, her chubby bare feet leaving faint impressions in the white sand beneath her as her white linen dress fluttered in the breeze.

CHAPTER TWO

"Rose, wake up! Baby, it's time to get up." Conroy nudged his wife as she lay buried under the bedding of their king-sized bed. "Paddington's ear is falling off, and Angie wants you to sew it back on, and Jake can't find his homework assignment. And--" he paused. "Don't forget you have your appointment today . . ." his voice trailed off.

Rose rubbed her eyes and cursed the sunlight. Of course she wouldn't forget her appointment, she thought angrily as she grumbled inaudibly under the covers.

"What did you say, baby?" he asked.

"Just give me five more minutes. *And don't call me baby!*" she snapped, the harshness in her voice had been mercifully muffled through the many layers of covers pulled over her face in an effort to block out the sunlight.

"You already asked for five more minutes *over fifteen minutes ago*! I need your help or I won't get the kids out the door in time for school," he insisted.

Rose groaned as she willed her body out of bed. Wild patches of strawberry-blonde fuzz protruded rebelliously from atop her head. She yawned, stretched, then started down the hall toward the kitchen. Angie had already poured herself a bowl of cereal, as was indicated by the trail of multi-colored donut-shaped clusters leading from the pantry to the kitchen table. Jake, apparently still on a quest to discover the whereabouts of his homework assignment, was frantically digging around in the family room.

The ordinarily tidy space was in a chaotic state of upheaval with overturned piles of magazines and paperwork, scattered seat cushions, and numerous other household items, which were all in varying states of disarray. Half of Jake's body was buried inside the toy box as he heaved items outward one at a time, up and over his head.

"Jake, honey, do you really think your assignment is in there?" she asked with amusement as she began calmly sifting through a pile of paper on the kitchen counter.

"I think Angie was playing with it last night," he claimed as his lower lip swelled in a pout. "She was coloring on the back of something, and I think it was my homework assignment," he accused with bitter conviction.

"Angie, is this true?" asked Rose, trying to appear stern for Jake's sake.

Angie shook her head in protest, her wide eyes expressing hurt and betrayal over her brother's accusation. Outside, the neighbor kids were already gathering at the bus stop. Rose glanced at the wall-clock in the kitchen, then upon returning her gaze, noticed something she hoped might be the object of Jake's quest. Moving quickly, she pulled at the corner of a piece of paper which she'd seen peeking out shyly from under the sofa. Jake's homework. Then, rushing to a drawer in the kitchen, she pulled out a bandage from inside and performed a quick-fix on Paddington's ear under the approving eyes of Angie. Next, she began rounding up the troops.

"Out! Now! GO, GO, GO, GO, GO," she called to them both, "or you're going to miss your bus," she ordered in the matronly voice she reserved for times such as this.

She stuffed the assignment in Jake's back-pack, told Angie to give Paddington a kiss goodbye, then patted them both on their backs as she affectionately pushed them out the door.

"Love you guys!" she hollered as they ran toward the bus, which would soon be pulling away from the curb, with or without her children. A little boy with red hair and freckles stood near the bottom step of the bus peering curiously at Rose in her bathrobe as she called out to her children to watch for cars. He smiled at her, then waved timidly to Angie and Jake as they boarded the yellow bus.

CHAPTER THREE

With the exception of an early meeting which she'd wrapped up by 10:30 AM, Cerise had cleared her calendar for the day. She methodically checked all her e-mails . . . nothing that couldn't wait until tomorrow, glanced at her empty inbox, then ran her manicured nails across the uniformly spaced piles of folders on her desk as she went through a mental check-list of what needed to be done.

Everything was in order. There was nothing pending which required her immediate attention. Flipping the switch to the Tiffany lamp on her mahogany desk, she collected her things and exited her spacious office with its impressive view of the Santa Monica skyline. On her way out the front door, she reminded her secretary she'd be out for the remainder of the day.

Cerise, an animal rights attorney, was presently embroiled in a lawsuit against the States of California and Nevada. Her client, the Equine Liberties Association, was doing their best to ensure she earned her keep on this case. She didn't mind though; she loved her work. She found fighting in court, while serving as a voice

for defenseless animals, to be an incredibly reward-
ing occupation. This was a high profile case, and she
felt certain this was her opportunity to finally make a
name for herself in the animal rights world.

Cerise, who had established a self-imposed agenda
for her personal success, was well within the projected
time frame for achieving many of her short-term professional and financial plans. Even now, many of her
long-term goals had already been achieved, or were
nearly within her grasp. She saw to it that nothing and
no one would come between her and her lofty ambi-
tions. She'd been in a few relationships with various
men over the past years, but had always made it clear
up front that any sort of commitment was not to be
expected. As far as she was concerned, commitment
was a death sentence for success.

Take Allen, for instance. He was sweet, but he was
clearly in love with her. And he wanted too much; far
more than she was willing to offer. She recognized the
signs all too well. Cerise knew it was time to end things
with Allen. He wasn't worth it; no one was when it
came to ensuring continued success and maintained
momentum where her goals were concerned. Allen was
just a hiccup, a speed-bump on the proverbial road of
her life, and he simply had to go.

Cerise had become quite adept at ending relationships. She could practically write a book on the subject
for all the experience she'd acquired over the years. The
key, she felt, was to remain cool and detached. As she
walked briskly down the hall toward the elevator, her
patent leather, red stiletto heels clicking smartly on

the marble floor beneath her, she made a mental note to end her relationship with Allen over the weekend. Tomorrow, she thought; I'll call him tomorrow and tell him it's over.

As she entered the elevator, a little boy ran in behind her just as the doors were about to close. Standing quietly in the opposite corner, the child fidgeted nervously, casting a sheepish glance in her direction. Ugh, kids, she thought, as she caught a glimpse of her ash blonde hair in the reflection of the elevator doors. Children were a distraction she most certainly did *not* need, she reminded herself as she smoothed a stray hair into place.

The little boy pushed a sandy blond ribbon of hair from his eyes and looked up at her with an impish grin. Cute--that's right, she reminded herself. Children were only endearing for a while. As with men, they could be amusing for a brief period of time, but what they really represented was a diversion, and that was exactly what she was looking to avoid in her life.

She pushed a button on the elevator panel, then shifted her handbag and began fishing around inside it. A moment later, she retrieved her cell phone, which she flipped open to check the LED clock on the screen. It was ten after eleven; she had just enough time to get across town.

Her stomach grumbled in complaint as a reminder that she hadn't eaten since the night before. As she returned her cell phone to her purse, she spied a granola bar. Pulling it out from beneath her wallet, she absent-mindedly started to tear at the wrapper, then, thinking twice, she pushed her emergency stash back down to the bottom of her bag. Later, she thought, as she impatiently waited for the elevator to stop. A bell chimed softly as the lift reached the basement parking level; she was outside before the doors had finished opening.

CHAPTER FOUR

Guy sat in an oak swivel chair at a large roll top desk in his home office. The handsome piece of furniture had once belonged to his grand-dad. He thought of his mother's father as he ran his hands across the work surface which was slightly worn and had been polished smooth from years of use. He inserted an iron skeleton key in a discreet compartment tucked away in a far corner. Giving it a quarter turn to the right, he heard a faint click as the door popped open, revealing a black velvet box.

He'd been searching for months for the perfect ring. He'd finally settled on this one, which he'd discovered at an eclectic little jewelry shop downtown which specialized in high-end estate jewelry. Reverently opening the black hinged box, he admired the ring with nervous anticipation. The wedding set he'd chosen was truly spectacular. But the sales lady had assured him, if Hanna didn't like it, they could come back and exchange the ring later. Still, he was fairly certain this was exactly what she would have selected if she had set out to choose one herself. The setting was elegant, yet classically understated, just as she was.

He hoped she wouldn't want a long engagement; he could hardly wait for them to begin the next chapter of their lives together as husband and wife. They hadn't actually discussed marriage yet; he was old-fashioned that way. He liked the idea of surprising her with a proposal.

So tonight, in celebration of their anniversary, he was going to give her this ring. They had been dating for exactly one year today, which might not seem long to some. But this relationship was different. Hanna was different. He felt as though he'd known her forever. From the day they'd first met, they both just seemed to sense that they belonged together.

Hanna and Guy had met at the shooting range; admittedly an unlikely place to meet a girl. She had been there to take a defensive gun safety course, and he was the instructor for the class. He had been immediately attracted to her big brown eyes and silky jet-black hair. But as the evening progressed, he'd been impressed by her good aim and steady hand, and she charmed him with her brilliant smile and quick wit.

That evening, following class, he'd asked if she'd like to join him for pie and ice cream at a little coffee shop around the corner. She accepted his invitation, and the two walked together to the cafe, where they proceeded to chat and laugh comfortably for hours as if they were old friends. Since then, they'd been dating exclusively.

He adored everything about her, her laugh, her

smile, the way she tugged at her earlobe whenever she got nervous. He knew without a doubt that he wanted to spend the rest of his life with her. He hoped she wanted a family and that she would want to get started right away. But if she didn't, that was fine with him; or if she wanted to wait, that was all right too. All that really mattered was that they begin their life together.

With her by his side, he'd have all he ever needed. Anything beyond that would be the cherry to his sundae. Hanna had actually brought up the subject of kids just the week before. It was a casual question, something about whether he'd ever thought about raising a family. But he was afraid if he talked too much on the matter, he might give away his plans, and he was determined to surprise her when he popped the question, so he had changed the subject right away.

Guy had spent countless hours working out all the arrangements to ensure everything about this evening would be perfect. He was taking Hanna to the *Point Vicente* Lighthouse where views of the setting sun were legendary. He'd ordered a simple meal to be prepared from her favorite deli, which he planned to stow in a picnic basket that he'd already packed with white linens and champagne glasses.

He'd even had a bottle of *Pierre Jouet* champagne custom engraved with the date, a sketch of the lighthouse, and the words *Will you marry me?* etched into the bottle. His MP3 player was loaded with a mix of their favorite songs so he could set the mood while they ate dinner overlooking the ocean and the spectacular view with the sun setting in the background. He wanted to take her breath away, and he was fairly certain this evening would do just that.

Hanna sat in her cubicle at work, gazing intently at a framed photo of Guy. It was a candid shot she'd captured a month earlier on a trip they'd taken to Yosemite. He was leaning against a large tree with an incredible panoramic view of *Bridalveil Falls* in the background. He looked handsome in a flannel shirt and two-day-old razor stubble, which he wore extremely well. With the captivating backdrop of the falls and Guy's natural rugged style, the photo looked like an image from the cover of an outdoor magazine.

Everything about Guy was solid, stable, and dependable. Since meeting him, Hanna had never had to worry about getting the oil changed in her car or cleaning out her rain gutters. He never presumed that she needed him to do these things, but he clearly enjoyed taking care of her. She loved that he respected her independence while still showing her that he could be chivalrous.

He was handsome, charming, and fun to be around, and she adored him. Ultimately, she hoped that he was *the one*. If he asked today, she'd say yes. But he'd never talked marriage, never even hinted for a moment that he might be looking for more out of this relationship.

They'd only been dating for a year now. But she knew that this was a forever kind of love. In a crazy sort of way, she often thought she'd have said yes the first night they'd met if he had asked.

At times Hanna felt as though things with Guy were almost too good to be true. She was afraid, nearly to the point of paranoia, that she might lose him. If only she could read his mind. She'd hinted just last week about whether or not he would ever want a family. But his response was evasive, so much so, she wished she'd never brought up the subject at all. In fact, since she'd asked him about his thoughts on kids, she felt as though he'd been more distracted. Why had she even asked? What had she been thinking? She should have just left things alone. She had him; wasn't that enough? The last thing she wanted was to make him feel pressured. She could wait until he was ready. In the meantime, she'd never do anything that might force his hand.

Hanna despised herself for being so insecure where Guy was concerned, but she'd dated her share of losers, and she knew a good thing when she'd finally found one. She simply would not risk messing up the good thing they had going. She was a strong, independent woman; and until he made it clear that he was ready for more, she would back off and give him the space he so clearly needed.

Lost in thought, Hanna was startled back to reality when her cell phone began ringing. "This is Hanna," she answered. It was Guy. A small smile slowly spread across her face. Independent, she reminded herself, detached, that was how she needed to be. Remain aloof, she thought. You can do this.

"Hey, pretty girl," Guy said in a voice that made her feel like she'd just been wrapped in a flannel blanket on a crisp fall day. "How's your morning going?"

Strong, she reminded herself, you are independent and strong.

"Great," she replied, hoping she sounded like she meant it.

"Happy anniversary," he said warmly.

Hanna shifted in her seat. Today was their anniversary? It hardly seemed possible that she could forget such a thing. She'd been so distracted over the last few weeks that she'd let that detail completely slip her mind. It was their anniversary; today, *of all days.*

Aloof, she told herself . . . stay detached.

"Happy anniversary," she returned after a moment's hesitation.

Guy paused, wondering if it was just his imagination or if something was wrong.

"So," he managed to say with a faint quaver in his voice. Had he detected something in her tone? He was only nervous about tonight, he thought, trying to convince himself that he was being paranoid. Snap out of it, man, he thought.

"I just wanted to remind you about tonight. I'll pick

you up at your office right after 5:00 so we can get an early start. Okay?" His heart was pounding now.

"Tonight?" she asked, her voice reaching an unexpectedly high pitch. "I . . . well . . . I . . . forgot," she said nervously as she tugged at her earlobe. "Oh, Guy, I'm so sorry. Really . . . I . . . things have been so crazy. I have an appointment and I don't know how late it'll be before I wrap things up. That, and I'm not feeling very well." It was only a half-lie.

CHAPTER FIVE

Pearl lay curled in a fetal position hugging a hot pink pillow as she rocked rhythmically to a song which was cranked nearly to full volume. Peering through damp, blood-shot eyes, her golden hair tossed wildly about her porcelain face, she watched the windows vibrate as lyrics blasted from the surround-sound speakers in the ceiling above.

Looking around her, she felt an odd sense of detachment as she surveyed the chaos and destruction which had come about as the result of her most recent outburst.

Minutes earlier, as she had searched for something to throw, she'd settled on a large mirror. Shards of reflective glass now lay scattered about, casting eerily fragmented images on the floor below. The pent-up anger and frustration she'd felt prior to her wildly destructive display had subsided minimally following the incident.

Over the past few weeks, she had become increasingly consumed by an ever-present sense of foreboding which had taken up residence within her. That cursed feeling often crept up on her slowly, gradually increasing in severity. At other times, though, it hit her with the force of a tidal wave, attacking suddenly and without warning.

Pearl knew it was just a matter of time before that overwhelming sense of dread would return in one form or another, wreaking havoc on her state of mind and her ability to reason. She found comfort, for now at least, in the fact that a mind-numbing ache had taken over. Aside from the likely possibility that she might at any moment vomit, she felt oddly better.

She knew her behavior during this recent outburst was puerile at best, but, damn it, her mother was impossible. Throughout her young life, Pearl and her mother had often been at odds. But lately she felt nothing but contempt for the woman who had given birth to her nearly eighteen years earlier. Pearl had always been resigned to the fact that, most likely, she and her mother would never be close. Today, however, as she contemplated her situation, she felt she truly hated the woman who was her only known living relative. As far as she was concerned, Ruby was merely the woman who gave birth to her. Pearl would never again refer to her as *Mom*. Ruby had lost the right to that title.

What kind of mother could do what hers intended to do--*to her own flesh and blood no less*? Words could not describe the anger, the sheer contempt she felt for her at this very moment. Pearl had thought about leaving. She had seriously considered taking her chances on the streets, but she had no idea how she would survive. She wished she were stronger, confident enough to stand up against her mom, but, regrettably, she didn't have the nerve to fight her on this. She didn't even know how. And for this, Pearl hated herself as much, if not more, than she did her mother.

Pearl surveyed her bedroom which would surely be the envy of most girls her age. With its trendy décor, hot pink walls, black and white accents and shag throws, it was the epitome of interior design. But those closest to her knew that this room, however fabulous it might be, came at a price. For all intents and purposes, it was a glorified prison cell.

Pearl had no doubt that, as a single mother, her mom worked extremely hard to support her. Ruby would never let Pearl forget that there had been days when she'd had to choose between keeping the electricity turned on and buying groceries. She swore she'd never allow her daughter to make the same mistakes she had made. Over the years, she'd made it clear to Pearl that she believed the only way to ensure that was to keep her daughter under close scrutiny at all times.

Often, Pearl had tried to imagine what kind of person her mother would have been under other circumstances. She envisioned a woman, much like her own mother, who had not known the strain of raising a child as a single mother. Would things have been different? Would she be warm, nurturing? Would she have been less protective and more loving?

Apparently, Ruby's own parents had never seemed too concerned with the choices she had made. According to Ruby, they had paid little attention to her whereabouts, who she ran around with, or how late she was out at night. So it had been no surprise to anyone who knew her when she announced, at seventeen years of age, that she was pregnant.

As she had often told Pearl, she blamed her own mother and father for their hands-off parenting style. If only they had offered her some guidance, if only they had provided her with boundaries, some sort of realistic expectations for a girl her age. That, Ruby had explained to Pearl, was the reason she was so hard on her.

For as long as Pearl could remember, her every move had been scrupulously dictated. She was permitted to have select friends over to the house now and again, but she was rarely allowed to venture out beyond the confines of school and extracurricular activities related to her musical endeavors. In particular, relationships with anyone of the opposite sex were entirely out of the question.

Pearl was never allowed to be in a position where possible errors in judgment might occur. On the rare occasion Pearl was granted permission to escape the confines of her home, she was expected to phone her mother the moment she got in the car to leave, again once she'd arrived at her destination, then periodically just to report in.

For most of Pearl's young life, she had desperately tried to earn her mother's trust . . . but to no avail. Apparently, it made no difference to Ruby that Pearl was a star student and an extremely talented cellist. It certainly didn't appear to matter that Pearl quietly accepted her mother's stringent guidelines without question, never balking at her mother's overbearing demands.

As a senior at the all-girls Catholic preparatory school which Pearl had attended since seventh grade, she had only a handful of friends. But there was only one girl Pearl's mother seemed to approve of, and that was Emily. Emily was Pearl's best friend, and she was the only person with whom Pearl could truly confide. She was also the only one who knew about the drama unfolding in Pearl's life.

Pearl dreamed of the day when she would finally be free of her mother. If she had any say in the matter, that day would come sooner rather than later. Given the choice, she'd attend college on the other side of the country. Ithaca would have been her first pick. But, as usual, her mother refused to hear her out on the subject.

Pearl had been playing the cello since the day after her fourth birthday. She couldn't remember a time in her life when she hadn't played. Over the years, her cello had become an extension of herself and music had become her one true form of expression. She excelled in orchestra, and despite the fact that she resented her mother for pushing so much, she truly enjoyed performing. She found solace in music, which provided a welcome escape, transporting her from an otherwise stifling existence. Her private instructors, along with her music teachers at school, all expected her to pursue a career in music.

For years, Pearl's mother had been researching conservatories across the country in an effort to determine the school which would best suit her daughter's academic needs. There were the obvious options like Harvard, Oberlin, Berklee, and Juilliard. But it came as no surprise to Pearl that her mother's first choice was Thornton Conservatory in Los Angeles.

As always, her mother intended to keep her nearby. If she attended school at Thornton, the commute would be minimal and Pearl might be stuck at home for another four years. Ruby had been lining up pre-interviews with a variety of B and C list schools over the last few months with the sole intent of having Pearl work the kinks and general nervousness out of her system before her interviews at the more coveted universities. But in the end, Pearl knew if her mother had anything to say about it, she'd be attending school at Thornton in the fall.

Pearl sat up in bed, her long legs folded in front of her as she contemplated her current situation. Per Ruby's orders, she was in lock-down mode. She knew she had screwed up. That, she would not deny. For all the many times she'd been obedient, subservient, the good child, she'd finally had enough. In a defiant act of rebellion, Pearl had openly and willfully ignored her mother's wishes. Just for once, she'd wanted to experience the thrill of spending time with a boy. Over the last few years, several had tried to earn her affection . . . more than her share. But she'd only ever felt a genuine attraction to one.

Adam had been enamored with Pearl since the third grade when she and her mother had first moved into the neighborhood. He'd started playing the viola just to be closer to her, and his plan had worked. Over time, she and Adam had become friends. And then a few months ago, things had gone a little farther than either of them had intended. It had been awkward. And later, they both admitted, they weren't ready for anything so serious.

Adam was a nice boy, but he was going away to college soon. She wasn't so sure what life held in store for her, but one thing she did know was that she wanted to start living. She knew there was a great big world out there, and for all the many years she'd spent being sheltered from it, she was anxious to get out there and devour it along with all it had to offer her.

Now that Pearl had finally attained a sense of calm, a small child named Ivory withdrew from her hiding place under the bed. Having been consumed with fear, the child had done her best to remain completely still during Pearl's outburst. Perhaps, she had told herself, if Pearl could forget she was there, maybe she wouldn't get so worked up.

She had never seen Pearl act out quite this dramatically and, quite frankly, the child was petrified. Ivory fully comprehended what Ruby was capable of. But Pearl; now that was another story. Until now, Ivory had been fairly certain she could depend on Pearl to look out for her, to take care of her, even if only for a short while. It had always been Ruby whom Ivory feared. But today, she wasn't so sure she could count on Pearl to protect her either. The child sat on the floor and hugged her knees to her body.

Please, God, she offered up a silent prayer, feeling lost and alone. *Help me*, she cried, hoping her prayer would not go unanswered.

As if suddenly remembering she wasn't alone, Pearl clenched her fists and started pounding on the bed.

"I hate you!" she yelled ferociously, causing the young child to shudder with fear. "You've ruined everything. This is all your fault!" she hollered hoarsely. "I wish you would just disappear and never come back. I hate you!"

Please, somebody help me! Ivory cried out in desperation.

CHAPTER SIX

Cerise pulled into the parking lot five minutes prior to her scheduled appointment. She gathered her purse, then paused for a moment as she contemplated bringing some work with her. On second thought, she reached for a recent law review from within her briefcase. She could catch up on a little reading while she waited. As she locked the door to her car, she smoothed the fabric of her double-breasted red suit. Her power suit, as she liked to call it, was the one she reserved for her most important meetings. This morning she'd had one such appointment. She was fairly certain she'd *wowed* her clients today . . . right on track, she thought.

She was plucked from her reverie when a disheveled woman approached her. Ugh, Cerise thought, this was a high end professional district. Why couldn't the city clean up their streets? The woman approaching her was wearing a thread-bare, gray dress covered in stains and torn at the hemline. She had the haggard look of someone who had been living on the streets for quite some time.

As she drew nearer, Cerise detected an offensive

odor coming from the same direction. She put the back of her hand to her nose to mask the stench and turned her back to the woman. She fished around in the side pocket of her purse and pulled out a stray twenty dollar bill.

"Here," she said, "go get yourself a meal," she offered smugly. "And a bath." She muttered the last part under her breath, all the while avoiding eye contact as she continued on her way.

"Oh no," the disheveled woman replied, suddenly appearing troubled, "I don't want your money." She glanced from side to side as if to see if anyone were listening. "But you could help me; would you please hold my bag for me? It would just be for a little while. It's gotten so heavy . . . heavier every day, it seems. I know it's not your problem, but would you mind helping me, just long enough so I can take a break from it?"

Cerise glanced at the black drawstring bag the woman was carrying. It appeared to be empty. "I can't help you," she said, almost feeling sorry for the woman.

The woman in the grey dress began humming. "Mm, mm, oh, so beautiful," she sang softly, "practically perfect in every way," she continued lyrically with her nonsensical melody. Her eyes glistened as her voice trailed off.

"My name's Achaia. What's yours?"

And you, my friend, are certifiable, Cerise thought, not bothering with a response as she stuffed the twenty back into her purse before making a hasty retreat. Cerise rushed through the double glass doors leading to the reception area where she was scheduled for her 11:15

appointment. In her haste, she nearly knocked over a tall potted plant. Glancing back over her shoulder to make sure she hadn't been followed by the crazy woman, she walked briskly toward the reception desk.

"Cerise LeRoux, here for my appointment," she announced with authority to anyone who might be listening.

One of the receptionists looked up briefly before collecting a stack of forms which she attached to a clipboard and slid in Cerise's direction. "Please fill out this paperwork, front and back," she droned methodically, without giving Cerise so much as a passing glance. "We're a bit behind schedule today. We'll call your name when we're ready for you," she said offhandedly as she gnawed on a piece of gum.

Cerise rolled her eyes. She could have stayed at the office a little longer and completed that brief she'd been working on. If there was one thing Cerise despised, it was failure on the part of others to stick to a schedule. She was a busy professional and expected to be treated as such. She had better things to do than to sit here, for who knew how long, waiting her turn to see the doctor.

Casting an acerbic glance in the nurse's direction, she took the clipboard and made her way over to a quiet corner in the reception lounge where she found a seat and began filling out her paperwork. A few minutes later she handed the clipboard and her completed forms to the receptionist before returning to her seat. Then she picked up her law review and began reading about recent lobbying efforts in the health care industry.

"Cerise? Cerise, is that you?" She glanced up to see a woman with strawberry blonde hair and hazel eyes looking at her intently. "Well, in a million years, I never thought I'd run into you here," the woman said.

"I'm sorry?" Cerise responded tentatively. "Do I know you?"

"It's me, Rose," the woman answered, sounding dejected. "We served together on the board of directors for the Equine Liberty Association a few years back. Only I was just coming on the board about six months before you were ending your term. So we never did get to work together much. How have you been?" she asked as if the two had been friends forever.

"Fine," Cerise responded, not feeling particularly chatty. She hoped this woman would get the picture and leave her to her reading.

"My, but that is a sharp suit you're wearing," Rose continued. "But then, you always did have such a terrific wardrobe," she asserted. "Now me, on the other hand, I just spend most of my time at home with the kids these days, so I don't bother much with suits and such," the plump red-head rambled. "My husband was going to come today, but I told him he needn't bother. I'm perfectly fine. Well, not perfectly," she stated nervously. "But it hardly seemed necessary for him to take time off from work, especially when he doesn't get that much time off to begin with. He started a new job about six months ago, and well, we're taking the kids to Disney World in a few months, and I'd hate for him to cut into his vacation time. The kids are so excited about going to Disney. Of course, they've been to Disneyland, but never to Disney World . . ." Her rambling continued as Cerise wondered if the woman would even notice if she went back to reading her magazine. ". . . and really, that's about all they ever talk about these days . . ."

Honey, come up for air! Cerise thought. She was fairly certain that at any moment the woman might keel over for lack of oxygen.

"Are you okay?" the red-head asked her, for what Cerise now realized had been at least the second time.

I've been caught, Cerise thought. I haven't heard a word she's said for who knows how long, and I have no idea what she's been talking about. "Sure, I'm fine," she responded. "Just not feeling so well," Cerise lied. She felt perfectly fine. But she needed an excuse for having tuned the woman out.

"Oh, look at me," Rose said in a fluster. "Here I am going on about myself, and I never even bothered to ask a *thing* about you. What have you been up to?" she asked.

Meanwhile, two young children eyed each other curiously as the red-headed woman continued to prattle, her unwilling audience exerting no effort to feign interest.

A little boy with blond hair stared intently at another boy with red hair and a smattering of freckles across his little nose. Following an extended silence, the blond boy spoke.

"My name's Ash. What's yours?"

"I'm Coal. My mom's Rose," came his timid response. Then, as if to put it somewhere for safekeeping, he hid his thumb in his mouth.

"My mommy has a 'portant job," Ash stated with great pride. "What does your mommy do?" he asked inquisitively.

Coal paused, pondering the question. Then, pulling his glistening thumb from his mouth for the briefest moment, he responded, "My mommy makes peanut butter sandwiches for my brother and sister. She cuts the crust off the bread," he announced as he puffed his chest out for emphasis.

"My mommy saves animals," Ash countered

"My mommy 'cycles plastic," Coal stated, not fully comprehending why he was engaging in this debate. But he was fairly certain his mother's honor was at stake, and he wasn't going to back down and allow the other boy a victory where his mother was concerned.

Rose continued, "So I started using the detergent they sell at the co-op. It's environmentally friendly, and they give five cents for every dollar to the Marine Life Protection Program. It's nice to know that my purchase can make a difference," she said wistfully. "And we all have a moral responsibility to protect our environment along with the creatures of the sea who would be lost without our help." She said it as though she were Sally

Muted Grey

Struthers, pleading with her viewing audience to help make a difference in the life of a child.

CHAPTER SEVEN

The trip across town seemed to last forever. Pearl sat in the passenger seat, her arms folded defiantly as her mother lectured.

"Life is all about choices," she said as she pulled the cap off a gold tube of lipstick, all the while keeping her eyes on the road. She twisted the base of the tube as a stick of bright red color emerged from within. Smoothing the color over her lips, she continued, "You know, Pearl, I'm not going to be around forever to help clean up after your messes. It's time you learned that, for every action, there's a reaction."

It was all Pearl could do to maintain her composure. One more cliché from her mother, she thought; just one more, and she might lose it! What she wanted at that moment more than anything in the world was to scream at the top of her lungs. She contemplated opening the door and jumping out as the car sped along the busy highway.

Her fingers toyed with the door handle as she envisioned her body being thrown out into a sea of traffic. If she was lucky, she'd be run over by a car. But what if she wasn't so fortunate? Her body could be tossed around like a pinball before traffic came to a stop.

Then they'd rush her mutilated body to the hospital, where an emergency medical team would work feverishly to save her life. Maybe she wouldn't be able to walk ever again, or maybe she'd be in a coma, trapped inside her own body as doctors probed her with tubes and various devices just to keep her in a vegetative state. That would make her mother happy, she mused; she'd have total control over her then.

Pearl slowly let go of the handle.

You're pathetic, a voice inside her head said. Pearl despised herself for being so weak. If she were stronger, she could do this. She could end it all right now, if only she had the nerve to open the door. But then again, if she were a stronger person, she'd be able to stand up against her mother. *You're pathetic*, the voice resonated.

"We're here," her mother announced cheerily, as if they'd just arrived at the parking lot of an amusement park. "Come on, honey, let's go," she finished in the same bubbly tone as before.

"What if I don't want to?" Pearl challenged. "What if I just said *no*?" she demanded, her arms still folded in defiance.

"Pearl, stop acting like a child," her mother ordered. "You get out of the car this instant young lady!" Ruby hissed, her perfectly painted lips pursed tightly as the woman came close to losing her composure.

Pearl got out of the car.

Fine, she thought, but that's it. As long as I live, I'll never speak to you ever again. As long as I live, as far as I'm concerned, you're just the woman who gave birth to me. And clearly, that act meant absolutely nothing to you. *I despise you!* She screamed the words in her head. The two women entered the building together in complete silence.

Ruby went to the front desk and announced their arrival to the receptionist.

"Here you go," a woman behind the counter said as she passed a dull-gray clipboard to Pearl's mom. "Damn pen," the nurse muttered under her breath as she looked down at her leaking pen. The red ink had stained her hands, spread to her lab coat and had even managed to bleed through to her blouse. She squirted a dab of sanitizer on her hands and began rubbing them together fiercely in an effort to remove the ink from her skin, but she didn't appear to be making much progress in removing the stain.

"Occupational hazard," she mumbled awkwardly. "It never does quite wash off," she quipped as Ruby smiled courteously before walking away, clipboard in hand.

Ruby turned toward the reception area where Pearl had already chosen a seat strategically wedged between two women, one in a sharp suit, the other, a red-head who quit talking mid-sentence when Pearl planted herself directly between them. With a dozen vacant seats available in the waiting room, the red-head looked stunned when Pearl had chosen this one.

Ruby, who was equally disturbed by Pearl's choice of seating, was resigned to sit in the next row over. A nearly imperceptible smile appeared on Pearl's otherwise sullen face.

Silence.

Ash and Coal sat together, quietly playing with imaginary airplanes, when a little girl sat on the floor beside the two boys.

"Who're you?" Coal asked bravely, before his thumb made a hasty retreat back to his little mouth.

"I'm Ivory," the little girl responded shyly, looking at the floor as she twirled her flaxen hair around a chubby little finger.

"Why are you here?" Ash asked the girl inquisitively.

The little girl refused to answer, shaking her head in response, her enormous brown eyes pooling with tears.

"I'm here 'cause I'm upside down," Coal said sadly.

"Nuh-uhh," Ash corrected the boy. "I just heard your mom say it's 'cause she thinks you might *have* downs."

"What's downs?" Ivory asked inquisitively.

"I dunno, but it must be 'portant, 'cause that's why I'm here, 'cause my mom's work is really 'portant," the boy announced proudly.

Muted Grey

"Cerise LeRoux?" a nurse called out as she searched the room for the next patient on her schedule.

It's about time! Cerise thought. Without a moment's hesitation she folded her magazine, stood, and began walking purposefully toward the nurse who was waiting by the door.

Great, the nurse thought; one of those high-and-mighty types. Over the years she had devised a little game to pass the time at work. It was her only source of amusement in this place she liked to refer to as the *cesspit*. The moment she'd spot a patient heading toward the exam room, she'd try and figure out their story. This one thought she owned the universe; that much was glaringly obvious.

The nurse thought back to the patient who had arrived earlier that morning, the girl in exam room number one. She hadn't even been able to play her little game with that one, because everyone working at the clinic already knew her story.

The young lady had been in here before, less than a year earlier, and before that, well, who knew how long it had been. But suffice to say, the girl spent far too much time in this office for anyone's good. Heck, she ought to get a punch card or something. The nurse snickered a little out loud when she thought of this.

The lady in the red suit glared at her. Well it was clear today was going to be a pretty dull day at the office. No sport to be had anytime soon, she thought as she led Miss High-and-Mighty to exam room number five.

CHAPTER EIGHT

Guy kept thinking and re-thinking his phone conversation with Hanna from earlier that morning. The more he thought about it, the more he couldn't help worrying. Maybe he had mis-read Hanna's signals. Maybe it was too soon. If she needed more time, well that was perfectly fine with him. He'd hoped they were well on their way to starting a life together. But what mattered most was that they were together.

He tried telling himself everything was okay, but if everything was fine, why was he having such a hard time convincing his stomach, which had been busy turning somersaults all morning? Something was gnawing at him, and he was fairly certain it had nothing to do with proposal jitters. It was a feeling he couldn't have explained to save his life, but something just didn't seem right. In fact, truth be told, something was terribly wrong, he'd bet his life on it.

Guy dialed Hanna's cell phone. The phone rang several times before going into her voice mail. She must be in a meeting, he thought.

"Hanna, this is Guy. Give me a call when you get

a chance," he said, hoping he didn't sound desperate. "I love you, pretty girl," he said into the receiver before hanging up.

Try as he might, he just couldn't stay focused. Work, it appeared, was entirely out of the question; at least until he could set his head straight. Pushing away from his desk, he decided to fix Hanna's night stand drawer. After she'd started sleeping over, he'd emptied it out for her so she would have a place to keep some of her things. The dresser was an antique and had scarcely been used in the years before Hanna had begun staying over. It was another heirloom passed down from his grandfather, and with recent use, the old tongue and groove had begun slipping on the front panel. Guy had been meaning to fix it before it got worse, or broke entirely. Now, he decided, was as good a time as any to get the job done.

He pulled the drawer out from the night stand and dumped its contents onto the bed before going out to the shop to get started on his project. In virtually no time, he had separated the tongue and groove assembly on the drawer. He sanded a few spots, then put a generous application of wood glue on the joints. Wrapping the finished edges with an old rag, he applied a vice grip to hold it in place. It would take a full day to dry properly, so he gathered Hanna's things off the bed and placed them on the dresser.

He was surprised to see Hanna's Day-timer in the pile of her things. She never went anywhere without it. She would, in fact, be lost without her calendar, she had said so herself on several occasions. He should take it to her. However, he couldn't recall if she'd mentioned where her afternoon meeting was. Opening the calendar to today's date, he saw, written in red ink with bold print: AFTERNOON OFF

Guy stared at the page in confusion. If Hanna had the afternoon off, then what was this meeting she'd referred to? It didn't make sense. Guy was doing his best not to over analyze the situation, but it was hard to ignore the facts which seemed to be shrouded in mystery.

Guy had always taken Hanna to be totally forthcoming; that was something he'd always appreciated about her. As far as he knew, they didn't keep any secrets from each other. So what was such a big deal that she felt the need to keep it from him now? Guy picked up the phone and dialed Hanna's number again. It rang twice before going to her voice mail.

Hanna arrived a few minutes early for her appointment. After stopping at the front desk, she took a seat in the crowded reception area. Perusing the selection of magazines on the side table next to her chair, she settled on an outdated copy of a pet magazine sporting an image of a golden retriever on the front cover. Maybe she'd go to the humane society and get a dog this weekend. The thought of rescuing a pound puppy pleased her as she flipped through the worn pages of the magazine.

Hanna heard her phone ring. It was the ring tone

she had designated for Guy. The phone rang twice before she pushed the power button, turning it off. She would speak with him later. For now, it was probably best if they didn't talk. Everything was going to be just fine, she told herself as she eyed a photo of an adorable Yorkshire terrier.

Grey, a little girl with chestnut-colored hair and eyes as black as the midnight sky, had entered the room just as Ash was saying goodbye to his new friends. As Ash and his mother left together to the examination room, Grey sidled in between the other kids and settled into playing a game which was already in progress.

CHAPTER NINE

Outside, as a steady stream of traffic buzzed by, Amaranth did her best to shimmy her car back and forth into the only parallel parking space available for over a block. Failing miserably in lining her car up with the curb, she admitted defeat and decided she was close enough.

She opened the car door and placed both feet on the asphalt before pulling herself out of her compact vehicle. She'd spent a good part of the morning lazing in the sun on the beach, and her legs had a hint of color now to show for it. She had thought her time on the beach might help clear her mind, but she still felt frazzled after her departure from Tad's house earlier that morning. She couldn't help but wonder if she was doing the right thing.

Amaranth walked willfully toward the double glass doors marking the entry of the clinic where she was scheduled for an afternoon appointment. As she approached the door, she was greeted by a scruffy looking woman who appeared to be in desperate need of a toothbrush and a bar of soap.

"Mmm hmm . . ." the woman hummed as if she were gearing up for a chorus of rousing gospel music.

"Flesh and bones
A river of life
A burden once may seem"
She chanted, as if in a trance.
"Stolen life
A breathe subsides
A choice, you may believe"
She continued as if speaking to no one. Yet for some reason, Amaranth was haunted by the words.
"Life deprived
Avoidance of strife
Forever uncertainty,
Regret, demise
You ought think twice
Or bear a haunting misery"

The final words were spoken with chilling conviction as the woman's frail voice trailed off into an agonizing moan.

Amaranth shuddered visibly, as if in doing so she might shake off the words spoken by the woman in the gray dress. Moving quickly to avoid further interaction with the woman, she tugged at the door. A blast of cold air hit her as she entered the building and headed toward the reception desk.

A nurse in a white lab coat greeted her with an

awkward smile and explained that they were a bit behind schedule. She handed Amaranth a clipboard and asked her to fill out the forms and return them to her once completed.

Glancing at a fresh spot of red ink on the woman's coat, she quickly turned away, still spooked by her encounter with the haggard woman in the grey dress. Amaranth took the clipboard and found a vacant seat in the crowded waiting room. As she filled out the forms, a little girl with curly blonde hair sat on the floor beside her.

Meanwhile, a number of children had now gathered in one corner of the reception room, and they beckoned the child with a halo of white curls to come join in their game. She only shook her head in response. Then, as if dismissing the other children, she hoisted herself to the chair above her and rested her head on her mother's lap where she began idly tracing the floral pattern on her skirt with a chubby little forefinger.

CHAPTER TEN

Upon determining that the rush in reception was finally under control, Fallun, the head nurse, returned discreetly down the hall toward exam room number one. She'd been listening for signs of disturbance from that direction since she'd moved up front to help out. More than likely, Dr. Edom hadn't made her way there yet, as she was probably still working with the late term procedure taking place in room four.

They had been behind schedule all morning since that Cain girl had shown up. It was all Clarice's fault. If she hadn't quit without a moment's notice, things would still be running like clockwork around here.

Clarice was too tender-hearted for this job. Fallun knew the type. People like her usually only lasted a week or so. Clarice had actually managed to make it three weeks; far longer than Fallun ever expected. Of course the girl had interviewed well. The new hires usually did. But all too often, on their first day at work, Fallun would begin to recognize the signs.

Most people simply weren't as thick-skinned as they might suggest during the interview, no matter how diligently she might try to explain the position and all it entailed. Until they experienced it first-hand, you never could tell. Then before long, they'd be calling in sick or offering other excuses for not showing up to work. Eventually they would quit, usually without much notice, just as Clarice had done.

By noon on her inaugural day at the clinic, Fallun had surmised it would only be a short while before Clarice would make a hasty and final departure from this place. Of course, the new front office assistant had chosen the busiest day of the week to walk out; go figure. The breaking point for Clarice had been the arrival of a patient who checked in earlier this morning. She was only nineteen years old, but had a file that dated back over four years.

The patient's name was Rory. The girl had first become pregnant when she was barely fourteen years old. She'd arrived then, frightfully young, naïve and very afraid. The next time she'd come to the office was on the day before her sixteenth birthday. Two years older, but none the wiser, she showed absolutely no remorse for having found herself in the same condition, twenty-some months later.

Her third visit to the clinic had clearly affected Dr. Edom. While the doctor had done her best to remain calm with the girl during the procedure, she'd caused a bit of a scene later when she began hollering at her, telling her to never come back.

When Fallun had pulled Rory Cain's chart from the rack on the wall that morning, she realized immediately what had happened. Clarice, the new receptionist, had failed to notice that Rory was on the 'black-list.'

Following her last visit, Dr. Edom had made explicit instructions that under no condition was this office to admit Rory Cain, ever again. Of course, to deny a patient access to treatment was a sticky situation. Now that Rory was here, Fallun wasn't quite sure they could ask her to leave. Quite frankly, she had no idea what to do with her.

Fallun chastised Clarice for failing to notice the enormous black dot on the Cain file prior to scheduling her for an appointment. The black dot, as Fallun had explained to the girl more than once during her training just a few weeks earlier, indicated that the patient had been black-listed.

As Fallun delighted in taking the opportunity to call Clarice every derogatory name she could think of, Clarice interrupted just long enough to announce she was quitting. Not at all set back by Clarice's pending departure, Fallun watched the young woman gather her things and turn in her key before she escorted her out the back door.

There'd be more like Clarice in her wake; *fresh blood*, she thought as she reminded herself to run an ad for employment by the end of the day. Then, since the front office had become congested with a number of not-so-patient patients, she hurried up front to help out. Finally, she checked on the Cain girl in exam room number one--still resting dreamily. At least, she thought, something was going as planned today.

For the last twenty minutes, as she was busily putting out fires, she'd also been putting off the inevitable. She knew she needed to inform Dr. Edom of the situation. She also felt certain the news would not be well received. She'd seen to it that Rory Cain was mildly sedated upon admittance, so hopefully the girl wouldn't be quick to notice any delay in her procedure. But time was running out. Eventually she'd need to reveal to Dr. Edom exactly who was awaiting treatment in room number one. But before Fallun could visit with Dr. Edom, she had one more patient who needed to be admitted for prep.

"Hanna Radcliff?" Fallun called out into the waiting room as a petite woman stood, returned a worn-out copy of a pet magazine to a table nearby and followed her to exam room number two. After asking a series of standard questions, Fallun handed Hanna a freshly washed and folded gown and asked her to change into it once she left the room. Pulling the door shut behind her, she then headed to Dr. Edom's office.

The doctor was at her desk writing prescriptions when Fallun tapped on her open door to announce her presence. Dr. Edom glanced in her direction, only offering her full attention after Fallun shut the door and took a seat. Fallun hated being the one to deliver unpleasant news; it was what she resented most about her job. The doctor had never been one to receive such reports with any amount of civility, so her reaction came as no surprise to Fallun.

"I want Clarice fired!" the doctor shrieked, sounding like a petulant child.

"Too late," Fallun responded soberly. "She already quit," the nurse finished. "What should we do about the Cain girl? She's already sedated and waiting for you in room number one," the head nurse reported.

"Rory Cain will just have to wait a bit longer. First I need to get back to our late term procedure in room four," Dr. Edom announced, her brow furrowed as she appeared to contemplate her options. "What I'd like to do is drop kick that smug little brat's sorry ass right out of here! If I never see her face again, it'll be too soon."

"Well, if that's all for now," Fallun trailed off, "I think I'll go check on the front office," she said as she turned and headed down the hall to reception, thankful for the excuse of limited staff to escape the doctor's wrath.

As Cerise lay on the table waiting for her sedative to kick in, little Ash toyed with his umbilical cord before he stretched and yawned. His tiny lips suckled aimlessly before he successfully navigated his thumb to his mouth. He knew so little of what might have become of him in a life outside the womb. But as he lay there, knowing that he would soon be exterminated, he pondered the life that would be taken from him.

With great sorrow, he accepted his fate, realizing he would never experience all those glorious opportunities he'd heard of and awaited with great anticipation. It just wasn't fair, he thought, as he realized he would never know the warmth of a mother's embrace or the sheer magic of watching with delight as snow shimmered and fluttered mystically in the lamp light. It hardly seemed possible that he would be denied his first steps . . . the nervousness and excitement of his first day of school.

Would his mother ever miss him? Would she ever wonder what kind of boy he might have become? Would she ever regret her choice? Then he wondered with trepidation, would it hurt to die when he had not yet been born?

A handful of children now remained in the waiting room. Coal and Ivory played together quietly for a while. Occasionally the two persisted in trying to get the little blonde girl across the room to join in their game. But with each attempt, she refused to leave her mother's side. Then, as the other children became engrossed in a game of I-spy, they all looked up in unison.

They had heard the nearly imperceptible sound of an agonizing moan. It was a child; that much they knew with total certainty. The sound was followed by an odd gurgling noise. Moments later, an ear piercing scream was heard by the children who now cowered in fear. Coal and Ivory instinctively covered their ears as looks of sheer terror crossed their faces. The little girl with the blonde hair clung to her mother's leg with all her might as she rocked back and forth, trying to drown out the sound while humming a tune in her head over and over again.

Finally, she gave in to her fear and began to cry. *Make it stop… Please somebody do something*! she cried in horror.

"Pearl Tacito?" a woman in a lab-coat stood at the doorway, calling for the next patient.

Pearl rose to her feet hesitantly, wishing she could be anywhere but where she was at that very moment.

Please, please don't make me go in there, a little voice pleaded. *I'm so scared,* Ivory clung fiercely to Pearl's leg. *Please*! she cried frantically as tears streamed down her little face. *Will somebody please listen to me*? she shouted until her voice was hoarse.

Outside, on the sidewalk in front of the clinic entrance, the woman in the gray dress sat huddled in a corner. Grabbing fists-full of matted hair, she pulled fiercely at her tangled tresses as she rocked back and forth, crying inconsolably.

"Make it stop . . . somebody make it stop!"

CHAPTER ELEVEN

Ruby tugged impatiently at her daughter's arm as Pearl proceeded haltingly toward the beckoning nurse.

In a matter of seconds, Nurse Fallun had adeptly sized up the situation with young Pearl and her mother. This was the classic case of a mother who'd somehow been deprived of the life she'd always dreamed of, who now hoped to live vicariously through her daughter. The mother insisted on micro-managing the poor girl to death to ensure the she had every opportunity for the perfect life. Hmm . . . funny the mom hadn't had a chastity belt put on her by the time she'd reached puberty.

The daughter, trying desperately to please a mother who simply couldn't be pleased, was miserable, going through her life feeling inadequate, unloved. In an act of rebellion . . . or no, Fallun corrected herself, in a desire to feel loved, the girl had turned to a boy. Now she was distraught over her situation, knowing she had sorely disappointed the woman whose love and acceptance she had tried to earn her entire life. She loved her mother, yet despised herself for loving a woman who wasn't capable of loving her back.

Now, feeling the need to please her mother, but resenting the woman for what she was forcing her to do, the girl was desperately confused about her feelings. An inconvenient situation this was. Typical story, Fallun mused. Fallun sided with the mother. Little brat, getting herself into trouble like this; what did she think was going to happen? Serves her right, she thought, feeling quite superior in her ability to judge.

"Which one of you is Pearl?" the nurse asked dryly.

"She is," Ruby responded.

"Can *she* talk?" Fallun asked with a sneer.

"Of course she can talk," Ruby replied incredulously, unaccustomed to being addressed with such disdain.

"And I suppose she's capable of walking as well?" the nurse continued, clearly enjoying putting Ruby in her place.

"What's your point?" Pearl's mother asked, obviously growing tired of this little game.

"The point is, you don't get to come along for this joy ride. We'll call you when your daughter is ready to go home. In the meantime, you're welcome to help yourself to coffee and cookies," she announced with a paper thin smile, dismissing the woman as she pulled the door shut behind her. She gave the handle an extra tug, waiting till she felt a click, indicating it was locked from the lobby side. Without another word, she led Pearl to the exam room.

As if in a daze, Pearl followed the nurse down the hall to the examination room at the south end of the clinic.

As Pearl arrived in exam room number seven, a terrified little girl named Ivory clung to her mother's leg, hoping against hope that her life might be spared.

"Fallun?" It was Dr. Edom. "I need you to take care of an incident in room number four."

"Right on it," Fallun said confidently. She knew exactly what Dr. Edom was referring to when she mentioned 'an incident.' Usually in order for there to be an incident, the patient had to be around twenty weeks, give or take. In those instances, the likelihood of a live birth abortion wasn't all that uncommon. The problem arose in what to do with the little imp. This was a child who should never have been born in the first place. Sure, there were now laws which protected the life of the infant, but when the father and mother wanted nothing to do with it, salvaging its life caused far too many complications. And of course there was the paperwork nightmare which ensued as a result of these unfortunate situations. *Not worth the headache*, she thought, as she headed down the hallway toward room four.

CHAPTER TWELVE

Dr. Edom realized she could no longer put off a visit to exam room number one. Now that she'd had some time to cool off, she intended to march in and announce to that girl exactly what she thought of her. Then, she would personally call her a cab, tell her to leave this office, and insist she never come back. Damn the repercussions; she simply would *not* perform another abortion on this girl. This was a respectable clinic, and she wouldn't have girls like Rory Cain coming in and destroying the image she'd worked so hard to maintain.

As she entered room number one, Dr. Edom was shocked to see the Cain girl sitting up, quite notably alert. The doctor glanced at Rory's chart, then down at her watch trying to assess how long it had been since the girl had first been sedated. As she returned her gaze toward the young patient's face, Dr. Edom was struck by the look of utter defiance from the girl who had already undergone three abortions before her eighteenth birthday.

Now, at the tender age of nineteen, Rory Cain sat

unabashedly on the examination table, wearing nothing but a light blue gown. Her posterior was partially exposed from the opening in the back of the gown, yet somehow she seemed perfectly comfortable sitting there with her little derriere prominently on display. The girl had a number of oddly positioned piercings protruding from her face, one over her left eye, two from her lip, and one on her tongue. Marah suppressed an overwhelming urge to slap her.

"So, Miss Cain, I see you still haven't figured out how to keep your panties on. I suppose I can take this to mean you also haven't learned a thing about the birds and the bees and their subsequent role in your frequent visits to this office?" As she said the words, her face became hot and she realized she was clenching her fists so fiercely her knuckles were turning white.

"Jus' cause you got that white coat on, don' make you smarter than me," the girl said with a sly grin as her head bobbed sarcastically from side to side. "An' I don' know what the hold up is, but you better quit draggin' yer feet an' speed things up, cause my boyfriend's gonna pick me up, an' he don' like ta wait," the girl announced defiantly as she placed both fists strategically on her hips. She was clearly enjoying this.

Marah felt a hot prickly sensation rising up her back. Until this precise moment, she'd always envisioned patients such as Rory Cain as girls who were desperately in need of her help. She'd been the one to come to their rescue. She liked to think of herself as a knight in shining armor, a Joan of Arc of sorts. But now, for the first time ever, her perspective began to shift, jarring her former perceptions, some of which were the very foundation upon which she had always justified her work.

In a sliver of a moment, she experienced a revealing glimmer of herself from the outside looking in. And from her new vantage point, the view was pretty horrific. Marah hated to admit that her job made it easier for women to throw caution to the wind, that it was she who cleaned up their messes.

With newfound acuity, she confronted her own acquiescence. In all her years of performing abortions, she'd carried out just a handful of procedures on women whose babies had been diagnosed with some form of illness, and sadly, in some of those cases, they'd later learned the initial test results had been inaccurate. And in the case of an abortion where a woman's life was at risk, not once ever had she performed such a procedure.

Yet day in and day out she performed abortions on countless women and girls. So where did that leave all the other procedures she'd performed? In all these years, she was aware of only one abortion she'd performed on a woman who'd been raped. And what of incest? No, she thought as she shook her head woefully; to her knowledge she had never terminated the life of a child who was the product of incest.

For the first time ever, she began to see the service she provided as a frightfully unsightly business, as though she were a glorified janitor of sorts. Only worse, her mop bucket was overflowing with the blood of the unborn. She stood awkwardly before the Cain girl, folding her arms in front of her body uncomfortably, as if to hide what was now exposed.

Marah had been so lost in her own thoughts, she'd nearly forgotten about the girl sitting on the examination table in front of her. As she glared intensely into the eyes of the young girl before her, she became furious.

"Abortion is not intended to serve as a form of contraception!" she hollered, her own face just inches away from Rory's. "If you think that's why I'm here, you're sorely mistaken!" As she spat the words, a smattering of spittle sprayed outward, misting Rory's cheek. The girl wiped her face with the back of her hand before using the same hand to swing round as her closed fist came directly into contact with Dr. Edom's jawbone, knocking her feet clear out from beneath her. As the doctor fell backward, her head crashed against the stainless steel instrument table before landing with a solid thud on the tile floor below.

Then why are you here? a voice in her head resonated as she lay on the floor with an array of medical utensils scattered about her, reflecting the bright lights from the halogen fixtures above. *Why exactly are you here?* Her body curled involuntarily into a fetal position.

As the doctor lay on the ground, shriveled in pain, her thoughts turned to the incident which had taken place in exam room number four just minutes earlier. During the abortion procedure, she had delivered a live baby boy. By her estimate, the infant must have been well over twenty weeks gestation. Of course, there were laws now which protected aborted fetuses who had endured the misfortune of being born alive. But that didn't make much of a difference here in the real world where she had a business to run.

Although it was rarely spoken of, as far as she knew many clinics chose to ignore such laws. So on occasions such as these, when an abortion went wrong and the baby was still alive, Dr. Edom left things in the capable hands of her head nurse, Fallun. As far as Dr. Edom was concerned, the less she knew, the better.

During her impressionable days as a student in med school, and for some time after, Marah had always understood a fetus to be a mass of tissue, and nothing more. But following her first late-term abortion in which the baby was born alive, she'd had to suppress some real doubts as to the validity of that claim.

Still, over the years, she'd become somewhat callous to the live births which occasionally took place during late term procedures. Meanwhile, she was providing a valuable service for those in need of assistance. And she took great pride in knowing hers was a facility which truly cared for the women and girls who relied on her and her highly skilled staff to help them during their time of need.

Her facility offered counseling by women who were genuinely concerned for the well-being of their patients. This year they had even begun offering an uplifting video of a clergywoman who helped allay the fears and concerns of those women struggling with the morality of abortion. Hers was a model facility, one which other clinicians spoke of with respect and admiration.

Dr. Edom had spent years suppressing a nagging feeling which had been insidiously gnawing away at her convictions. But now, with the Cain girl staring down at her from her perch on the examination table, Dr. Edom had come face to face with the brutal truth.

Rory Cain was not an exception; she was in fact the archetypal patient of this clinic. Albeit, many weren't quite as young; most weren't as openly defiant or confrontational, but nearly all were here for her to clean up after their messes. And she had been an eager participant in their endeavors to sweep their problems away; out of sight, out of mind.

As Marah ruminated upon thoughts she'd attempted to suppress for so long, the throbbing in her head became unbearable. With both hands, she compressed her skull, trying in vain to keep the pain at bay. As her head began to spin out of control, she squeezed her temples mightily, as if to force her misery from settling into her cranium.

As darkness closed around her, Dr. Edom found herself in a place she knew all too well. It was the place of her dreams, the world she seemed never able to escape. She was being thrown from a horse, his evil eyes taunting her as he reared, tossing her into the blood-red surf. She felt the arms of the sea pulling at her.

Only this time she realized it wasn't a body of water at all; she was surrounded by the countless women upon whom she'd performed abortions. They were wailing

and gnashing their teeth. Some appeared to be remorse-
ful. Others, with their haughty sneers, clearly proud of
the choices they had made, looked at her in contemptu-
ous defiance. The blood of thousands of unborn babies
sloshed around her as the sticky red matter covered her
hands, her face, her hair.

And then she heard the cries of the unborn. Why? Why
did you kill us? We were so full of life. We had futures,
opportunities, dreams, all stolen from us. How could you?
You knew! You held so many of us in your hands, some
of us while we were still breathing. Are we so different
from those children who are born prematurely to moth-
ers and fathers who cling to the lives of their babies, those
whom doctors will do anything to save? How are we any
different? From the moment we were conceived, we were
miraculously formed . . . divine gifts.

How could you choose to deny it? Our tiny beating
hearts, our little fingers and toes; we were the lives of the
innocent. But we were silenced before ever we found our
voice. Had we not been mute, we would say emphati-
cally, we choose life! But our wishes have been denied, all
in the name of another's entitlement to choose. We were
not given the choice. We have been murdered, plain and
simple. How did the lines ever become so faded? Those
lines which were once so clearly black and white have
bled together; now they are nothing more than a muddy
shade of grey. Yet, despite your insistence upon spurning
our existence, the truth remains.

Marah began gasping for air, her head bobbing on
the surface of the crimson sea. Choking on the blood of
the unborn, she realized she would soon suffocate, as

slowly, torturously, the women began pulling her down with them, deeper and deeper into the throes of hell. And then, just as she thought she'd taken her last breath, she pleaded for mercy.

"Please, I know I don't deserve it. I know that I, of all people, am not worthy of your forgiveness, but please God, let me make it right!" Her thoughts trailed off as surely, she surmised, she must be dying. Undoubtedly it was too late for her; too late for atonement, too late for mercy, too late . . .

And then she saw an incredible light from above, the brilliance of which was nearly blinding. She felt overcome by peace and love and an unexplainable, yet undeniable, ethereal sense of joy.

CHAPTER THIRTEEN

Guy tried to find something to busy himself; anything to get his mind off the conversation he'd had with Hanna earlier that day. But he just couldn't avert his mounting concerns which now seemed to consume his every thought. Putting his phone on perpetual re-dial, he persisted unrelentingly in an attempt to reach Hanna. Finally, not knowing what else to do, he dialed her sister's number.

"Kelcey, this is Guy," he said with a catch in his voice, hoping she wouldn't detect the panic he was trying so desperately to conceal. "I can't seem to reach Hanna on her phone. I've been trying her all morning and it's really important that I find her. Do you have any idea where she might be?" he asked with as much calm as he could muster.

Kelcey stammered, "I, I, I'm not sure." She was clearly caught off guard by his unexpected call.

"Kelc, I know something's up. Please just tell me," he pleaded, no longer attempting to hide the desperation in his voice.

Kelcey hesitated. Then, ultimately, no longer willing or able to withhold her sister's secret, she began to clamor.

"I told her she should tell you, that she should talk to you first, but she was afraid of how you might react." She sounded as though she were about to cry.

"What . . . why? Kelcey . . . where?" He could barely control the trembling in his voice as he attempted to verbalize his thoughts.

Then, before Kelcey could respond, he realized he already knew the answer to his fragmented questions. As the agonizing truth surfaced, he groaned audibly. Last week, Hanna had been trying to ask him whether or not he wanted children. He'd been evasive. How could he have been so stupid? At the time, he'd been afraid he might give away his surprise. After all, it would only be a week, then they'd be engaged, and they would be talking all about their plans, their future, and the possibility of a family. Could it be? Was it possible that she was carrying their child?

"She's at the abortion clinic in Santa Monica," Kelcey sputtered, as she choked back sobs. "I know where it is," she paused, trying to gain control of her erratic breathing which was now coming in short ragged gasps. "I'm supposed to pick her up there in an hour. I'm so sorry, Guy. She made me promise not to tell," she cried as she frantically pleaded with him to go at once and stop Hanna from doing the unthinkable.

Guy was already in action. Assuring Kelcey he'd stop at nothing to keep Hanna from going through with the abortion, he got the address to the clinic from her as he grabbed his keys off the counter. Then as an afterthought, he rushed back and snatched a camouflage back-pack off the floor beside his desk. He slung the strap of the pack over his shoulder, then hurried out to his SUV and squealed out of the driveway as he headed toward the clinic which, mercifully, was just a few miles from his home.

Minutes later Guy pulled his vehicle into the clinic parking lot. Realizing there were no parking spaces available, he double parked behind a red convertible, then ran around to the front of the building where he hastily entered the glass double doors at the main entrance. A woman in ragged clothes looked at him and shook her head woefully as he rushed by.

At the front desk, Guy was met by a nurse in a lab coat which bore a red ink-stain on the pocket, its color bleeding through to her partially exposed blouse beneath it.

"Can I help you?" she asked, one eyebrow was raised inquisitively.

"I'm here to see Hanna Radcliff," he said, his heart beating so intensely he could hear his blood rushing.

"I'm sorry, are you here to pick her up?" the nurse asked condescendingly. "Because she won't be ready . . ." she paused as she glanced at the schedule on her desk, clearly in no hurry to help him out, ". . . for another 45 minutes. You're welcome to wait over in the lounge. Please help yourself to some cookies and coffee," she said, her lips turning up at the sides in a smile that seemed to mock him.

"You don't understand, I need to see her *now*," he insisted.

"I'm afraid that isn't possible," the woman said with a sardonic smile.

Sensing he was losing valuable time, Guy turned and rushed toward the only door he could find that might lead him to Hanna. It was locked. Glancing around nervously, he realized this door was the only public access to the examination rooms in back. Guy impulsively ran back outside toward the parking lot. He pulled frantically at a door he'd noticed when he'd first arrived. It had the name of the clinic in small bold-faced type, followed by the words EMPLOYEE ENTRANCE. The door was locked.

"Agh!" he grunted in exasperation as he slammed his open palm on the brick exterior of the building before rushing back to his vehicle.

Amaranth sat in the waiting room, absent-mindedly flipping through the pages of a magazine, lost in introspection. A small contented smile spread slowly across her face as she thought of Tad and the good times they'd shared together. Despite all that, she felt she had made the right decision about their relationship. It was time to move on.

She was ready to admit that he'd never been a healthy choice for her. Maybe it had been an avoidance issue with her. Maybe in an effort to stay young and care-free, she'd strapped herself down with the one person who would never be able to commit. In retrospect, there were things she'd learned from the relationship. While being with Tad hadn't necessarily been the best choice for her, she was glad to have known him, for whatever it was worth.

And now, here she sat, with his baby growing inside her. What a bewildering thought . . . to know that her body was harboring a little life, and that this living thing was a part of her, a part of Tad. How big was it? And what was it? Maybe it was a little boy with sandy blond hair like Tad's; or maybe a girl, with bright blonde curls like her own. Did it know what she was thinking? Did it know of her plans to put an end to its life?

For the first time, Amaranth tried to envision the baby in her womb. She knew it wasn't really a person yet. At least that was what the clinician had told her during her initial appointment. But somewhere in the back of her mind she wasn't so sure. As she contemplated the infant within her, she began to think of the miracle of life, from conception to birth. What a privilege, what an incredible experience it would be to help bring a child into the world.

She wondered why it had never crossed her mind before to keep the baby. Perhaps it was because she knew Tad wouldn't want it. A baby would certainly be a hindrance to his otherwise carefree lifestyle. Well, so what, she thought. He didn't have to raise this child; neither did she, for that matter. She'd had friends who'd been on waiting lists for years to adopt a baby. She could find a loving couple to raise their child. Or . . .

And then Amaranth thought of her two bedroom condominium. Over the past few years, she'd spent far too little time there, but it would be a wonderful place for her baby's first years. Eventually, maybe she'd settle down in a quiet little neighborhood, one with a good school, close to work. Either way, she had time to decide; nearly eight more months. Wow, she thought, eight months and I'll be able to meet this little life, this tiny person forming inside me.

Amaranth didn't know at what point she had stood up and begun to exit the clinic. All she knew was that she was already making a mental list of what needed to be done. Her heart was pounding so quickly she thought it might burst. And she felt good. She felt really good.

Oblivious to everything else going on around her, she walked out the door with a radiant smile on her face. The sun was shining, there was a light breeze, and she was greeted by the crazy lady again.

"And what's your name, you lucky girl?" the woman asked, looking in her direction.

Amaranth looked around for a moment, then hesitated before responding. "I'm Amaranth," she stated cheerfully with a light-hearted giggle, "and why do you say *I* am so lucky?"

"Not you. I was talking to her . . ." the crazy lady responded, somehow not sounding so crazy after all. Amaranth looked around again, but still didn't see anyone else in the vicinity.

Choice, came the sweet soft voice of a little blonde child. *My name is choice.*

The crazy lady smiled in response.

Amaranth returned the smile before walking toward her car with newfound determination as she continued to think of all the things she needed to do. A list, she thought. *I need to make a list.*

She was briefly distracted from her reverie when a tall man, who appeared to be in a colossal hurry, nearly ran her off the sidewalk as he rushed toward the building from which she had just departed. Amaranth was in far too good a mood to even notice the man as she buoyantly continued on her way. As she walked, a little girl named Choice skipped joyfully beside her, humming a happy tune.

CHAPTER FOURTEEN

On his way in, Guy could hear the woman in the tattered gray dress saying, "Go get 'em!" as she looked at him with admiration, giving him the thumbs up sign.

Once inside the double doors, he smoothed his hair, steadied his breathing, and walked calmly toward the locked door leading to the exam rooms. Then he took a seat in a vacant row of chairs, strategically selecting the one nearest the door. A moment later, a nurse stepped into the waiting room and called out for the next patient. "Amaranth Linde?" she announced, waiting for someone to stand and begin walking in her direction.

Guy stood calmly and approached the nurse. Then, so only the nurse could see, he pulled out a pistol. It wasn't loaded, but no one needed to know that. The nurse's smile quickly faded.

"Hanna Radcliff; where is she?" he asked in a husky whisper, pointing the gun directly at the nurse who was standing between him and the exam rooms. "Take me to her now," he asserted in a hushed voice, as a mist of perspiration formed on his upper lip.

Head nurse Fallun nervously escorted Guy toward Hanna's room. She stopped at the nurse's station pretending to look up the room number. Then as the two started toward Hanna's room, the nurse quickly pressed a silent alarm button hidden discreetly on the underside of the counter which was programmed to send a distress signal to the local police department.

A moment later, when they arrived at her room, they found Hanna lying on an exam table wearing a pale blue gown. Guy could hardly believe how beautiful she looked lying there with her hair floating around her face. She was sedated, that much he could tell by her blank expression. After a moment, her eyelids fluttered and she looked around, as if trying to make sense of what was going on.

"Guy?" she asked, clearly confused. "Why? How did you? Where's . . . Kelcey . . . ?" her voice trailed off. She seemed to be trying desperately to focus on him . . . to make sense of the situation.

"Out!" he said to the nurse, pointing the gun directly at her face. Fallun scurried out the door, knocking over a jar of swabs in her haste. The glass jar fell to the ground and shattered. The metal lid flew off and began spinning like a shiny penny on the tile floor below. Guy locked the door behind her and slid a cabinet in front of it for good measure. He knew it would only be a matter of minutes, at best, before the police would arrive. He just wanted some time alone with Hanna before everything got crazy.

Crazy, Guy thought; talk about crazy. He hadn't

even thought about what he was going to do next. All he knew was that he'd needed to get to Hanna in time. And now, here he was. He could only hope he wasn't too late.

Dr. Edom blinked several times, trying to focus on . . . was that the ceiling? She reached for the back of her head which was throbbing and inexplicably tacky to the touch. What was she doing on the floor? She vaguely recalled an altercation with the Cain girl. And then with a sudden jolt of clarity, she remembered the dream. It *had* been a dream, *hadn't it?* She was startled back to reality when she heard the sound of breaking glass coming from the adjacent room. She struggled to pull herself up, glancing for a moment at the young girl sitting on the table above her. The girl was looking down at her with obvious amusement, her legs dangling childishly above the doctor's head. Did that smirk never leave her face? Marah wondered incredulously.

"Stay here!" she barked at the girl as she pushed herself up from the ground, willing her reluctant body into motion. Holding her aching head in her hands, she stumbled out of the room just as head Nurse Fallun was fleeing exam room number two. In Fallun's haste, she collided with Dr. Edom, who was still in a state of shock.

"I've activated the silent alarm! The police should be here any minute. We need to evacuate the building!"

Fallun said frantically as she looked around, wide-eyed, as if expecting something catastrophic to happen at any moment. The doctor stared, dumb-founded.

"It's really not such a big deal," Dr. Edom said acerbically, thinking Fallun had gravely overreacted. She was perplexed as to how the nurse could have learned that the Cain girl had assaulted her.

"Oh really?" one of the lab technicians asked. It was more of a statement than a question. She, along with a handful of other employees, had gathered after hearing all the commotion. The lab technician had one hand on her hip and was studying the doctor inquisitively. "By the way, did you know you're bleeding?" she finished defiantly as she opened a first aid kit on the wall and produced a handful of antibacterial wipe pouches. Tearing one of the packages open, she began wiping at the blood on the back of Dr. Edom's head.

"Okay, let's start over again. And slow down this time," Marah demanded as she batted the woman's hand away from her head. "What's going on here?" she asked, more than a little confused.

CHAPTER FIFTEEN

"Is it?" Guy stammered. "Am I?" He couldn't bring himself to say the words. "Am I too late?" Tears formed in his eyes as he asked the question. A metal lid spun wildly, causing a riotous commotion before warbling to a complete stop on the cool hard floor, the sound resonating like a crashing cymbal.

Hanna looked up at him, not knowing what to say. *What had she done?* She moved her head from side to side, her reddened eyes pooling with tears. As her body began to shake, she placed a quivering hand over her mouth, unable to speak. Guy put his head in his hands and moaned the agonizing sound of a wounded animal.

She covered her ears and cried out, "Oh my God-- what have I done? *What have I done?*" her voice becoming more jagged and raspy with each utterance.

Guy pulled a little black box out of his pocket. He'd been carrying it around with him all morning. He caressed the soft velvet of the box, then slowly lifted the lid. For a moment, he stared blankly at the contents, then with finality, he snapped the box shut.

After tenderly touching her abdomen, he removed his hand, and set the box in its place. She felt the departure of his warm hand, followed by the coolness of the little black box. Then an indescribable emptiness arose within her, the ache of which seemed more than she could endure. Hanna looked pleadingly at Guy, but the hurt in his eyes spoke volumes. His were the eyes of a grieving man.

"I got that for you, for us, for our future," he stated blandly. "But we don't have a future now. You can have it. I don't know what I would do with it." And with that, he turned and slid the large cabinet out from in front of the doorway just as the police SWAT team was pulling into the parking lot outside, leaving a trail of fresh tire marks as it screeched abruptly to a halt. The door of the van was already sliding open long before the van had come to a complete stop. Six men in tactical assault gear jumped out and charged the back door of the clinic.

Guy unlocked the door and slowly began to walk into the hallway as several armed men rushed in and surrounded him. With one hand above his head in a show of surrender, he put the gun on the floor in front of him. Then he put his other hand in the air as two of the men grabbed him and slammed him against the wall. The other four stood motionless, pointing their guns strategically at Guy to thwart any attempt at escape.

Dr. Edom looked on in shock as Guy was handcuffed, then escorted out the back door toward the police van amid bright bursts of light from flashbulbs as members of the media tried to catch a shot of the man who had wielded a gun in an abortion clinic.

CHAPTER SIXTEEN

Pearl had sat in silence for what seemed like an eternity, waiting for someone to prep her for her procedure in exam room number seven. As she waited, she began thinking about her life, her future, and about the life growing inside her. It still didn't seem possible that she was carrying a child. Pearl knew she wasn't ready to be a mother. But she also knew, with sudden clarity, that she did not want to spend a lifetime regretting this day and the choice she had nearly allowed someone else to make for her.

Things had happened so quickly, that they hadn't had a chance to follow standard emergency protocol. Now that the assailant was in custody, Fallun went out into the lobby to apprise everyone of the situation. She announced that a man had entered the building with a gun, but had been removed by the authorities without any resistance. She promised them that everyone was perfectly fine and that they would soon be reunited with their friends and loved ones.

An officer briefly investigated the incident, collecting the names of everyone who was in the building that day so he could follow up later with any further questions. After the officer cleared everyone to leave the building, Fallun made a brief announcement, explaining it would be necessary to reschedule all remaining appointments for the day.

"Fine," Ruby responded, her shrill voice rising above the murmurings of others in the room. "Can you please tell me if my daughter's procedure has been completed yet?" she asked, as if absolutely nothing out of the ordinary had just taken place.

The nurse was shocked by the woman's single-minded determination. "*No*, it has not," she said, firmly. "Now if you'd like to come with me, we can get your daughter's appointment rescheduled."

"Oh, that won't be necessary. We can just wait until everything settles down here. No need to reschedule," the woman announced with feigned authority.

"Did you hear anything I just said?" Fallun asked incredulously.

"Of course I did, but we can wait," was Ruby's cool response.

"Excuse me, but do you realize all our lives were in jeopardy today? I can't believe you're taking this so lightly. A man pointed a gun at my head for God's sake!" Fallun said with a trembling voice.

"If I were you I'd be thankful he showed you more mercy than you deserve. Tell me, how many babies died here today?" It was Pearl's young voice, cool and confident. She had changed into her street clothes and entered the lobby just in time to hear the exchange between the two women.

"Exactly what do you think you're doing Pearl?" Ruby asked, clearly displeased that her daughter seemed to think they would be leaving any time soon.

"What I should have done earlier," the young girl said decisively, refusing to back down to her mother for the first time in her life. "I called Emily and she's on her way to pick me up."

"For God's sake, Pearl, you're just a child. Do you really believe you know what's best for you right now?"

"Yes, I do," Pearl said as she shifted her purse over her shoulder and started toward the door. "And if you so much as say a single word to try and stop me, I'll notify the police. Then you can explain to them how you tried to force me to murder my baby."

Ruby was stunned into silence as she stood, mouth agape, witnessing her daughter's defiant departure.

CHAPTER SEVENTEEN

So there was a little sport to be had today after all, Fallun mused, as she said goodbye to the other nurses and went out front to water the flower beds before heading home for a slightly extended weekend. As she did, she was greeted by that blasted crazy woman who never seemed to stray far from the front doors of the clinic. They'd tried in the past to have her removed by the authorities, but to no avail since she wasn't panhandling, and she didn't appear to be a threat to anyone. But Fallun was always unnerved by her encounters with the woman.

"Hi, Nurse Ratched," came a hackle from the woman in the tattered gray dress. "Did you have a nice time killing little babies today?"

Fallun tried to ignore the woman who had long ago become a thorn in her side.

"Will you carry my bag for me?" she asked Fallun, referring to a black drawstring satchel which she wore slung over her back. "It's so heavy. I can't bear the weight of it anymore," she said imploringly.

Usually Fallun ignored the woman's rantings, but

after the day she'd had she was feeling agitated, so she toyed with her just for spite.

"Achaia, you know there's nothing in that ridiculous bag of yours. It's been empty for as long as I've known you--ever since I started here at the clinic. You've been complaining about that empty thing for years now. Why don't you burn that old thing, give up your post here, and get a life?"

"I know it's empty, Nurse Ratched. You think I don't know that? That's exactly why it's so heavy," she said somberly, as if this acknowledgment made perfect sense. "I gave it all away, but it wasn't mine to give-- treated it like it was trash, but I can't get it back now; can never get it back . . . oh, the excruciating weight of it," the woman began sobbing as she dropped the empty bag to the sidewalk as if it contained a ton of bricks. Then she began feeling around inside the bag, frantically searching for something which she most certainly would not find inside.

Fallun shook her head in disgust as she walked toward her car which was parked in the lot behind the building. She'd had enough of this place for one week.

Dr. Edom had sent all the staff members home early. Now, in solitude, she wandered down the halls of the small private clinic she'd operated for nearly half a decade. She began switching off all the lights in the building, starting up front and working her way toward the back.

How had she done it all these years? How had she managed to shut off her ability to reason? And at what point had she finally known? It must have been years now; surely she must have known from the time the dreams had begun. Those feelings she'd attempted to suppress during the day had been forcing their way into her consciousness at night.

For the first time in all these years, she finally acknowledged the truth. She was a murderer. She took the lives of innocent babies, all for the sake of convenience. She did this so that countless women, who couldn't be bothered with any sort of disruption in their own lives, could carry on, living, breathing, and enjoying the freedoms bestowed upon them; freedoms their own babies would never know.

She began to sob. Leaning back against the wall in the dark hallway, she slid down until she was huddled on the ground. She hugged her legs as her body shook, and she cried . . . tears for the lost.

Marah had no idea how long she'd been sitting on the clinic floor when she realized someone had left a radio playing somewhere in the office. She got up and followed the sound which appeared to be coming from inside the utility room. Why, she wondered, would there be a radio in the utility room?

Curiously, she opened the door and pushed the off button to the small boom-box which rested on a shelf above the hazardous waste bin. Then she stopped and held her breath. To her horror, she realized a muffled sound was coming from within the large plastic receptacle used for discarding bio-waste. Lifting the lid, with mounting trepidation, she stared inside as she discovered the source of the sound she'd just heard. There, covered in blood and amniotic fluid, was the baby boy born earlier that day. He was the incident which Dr. Edom had asked Fallun to handle.

So this was how Fallun handled these situations? What kind of monster could leave a baby to suffer a slow and agonizing death such as this? Marah held her breath as she swallowed back the urge to vomit.

Me, I'm *that* kind of monster . . . she acknowledged. As she looked on, with horror, at the dismembered shards of the lives she'd taken that day, her hands began to shake uncontrollably.

She was startled back to reality when she heard a whimper from the infant. The baby, covered in a white waxy substance, was still attached to the placenta, his umbilical cord running from his belly to the small parcel on which he lay.

Although he was still breathing, the undertones of his skin were purplish-blue, indicating he'd been slowly suffocating from lack of oxygen. Finally, as if a cloud of fog had been lifted, Marah realized she needed to act quickly. Retrieving the baby from the dumpster, she wrapped him in a lab coat to keep him warm, then she held him in her arms as she rushed to a phone and dialed 911.

Muted Grey

After the paramedics arrived and took the baby away in an ambulance, Marah decided to take a walk around the building. She had a lot of thinking to do. She didn't know if she'd be returning to the clinic ever again.

As she rounded the corner to the front of the building she thought back to the day when she'd signed the lease on this building, the day she'd committed to starting her own private practice. Marah could remember thinking what a fine building it was; hadn't it been white back then? How then had it turned such a dingy shade of grey? Had the smog had such an effect on the paint? Or had she just remembered it wrong?

Marah was drawn from her reverie when she was greeted by Achaia, the resident crazy lady.

"Will you carry my bag for me?" she asked Marah. "It's so heavy, it's hurting my back. I can't bear the weight of it anymore," she said, crying as she did.

"Achaia, you know there's nothing in that satchel. It's time you let it go."

"You did a good thing today," the woman in the gray dress said to Marah.

"Maybe," Marah said, pondering the events of the day. "But that will never make up for all the harm I've done," she finished, wondering if she could ever find forgiveness for the choices she had made.

"Can I give you a ride somewhere, Achaia?" she asked as she reached out to take the tattered old bag from the woman. Achaia hesitated for a moment, then with a nervous sigh, she gently released the bag.

"Ahhh," she exhaled. "I never imagined that could feel so good." A hesitant smile appeared on her weathered face as Achaia spread her arms outward. Slowly, she began spinning around. As she gained speed she began to laugh. Looking upward into the sky, tears of joy streamed down her face which now reflected pure radiance from the sun up above.

THE END

EPILOGUE

Pearl sat in the living room at her friend Emily's house where she was working on an audition piece. Emily's mother had agreed to let Pearl stay with them for as long as she needed. The plan was that she would stay until college started in the fall. She had applied to attend Ithaca and was hopeful that she would be accepted.

With Emily's mother's help, she had contacted an adoption center which had paired her up with a family who desperately wanted a child. Pearl had met the couple, felt a genuine connection with them, and was thrilled when they agreed to an open adoption. She looked around the room and smiled, feeling good about where her life was heading.

Pearl's slender legs framed her cello as she began to expertly coerce its strings. A fine dust of rosin floated through the sunlit air as she played the first measure of *Brahms' E minor Sonata*. She closed her eyes, moving with the rhythm of the music, her long golden hair swaying in sync with each perfectly timed stroke of her bow, her hand pulsating as she coaxed a resonant vibrato from the strings. So hauntingly beautiful was the piece that Pearl was moved to tears as she began playing the second movement.

Exactly fourteen weeks earlier, another teardrop had fallen from her face onto the antiqued maple of her cello, leaving a spot where specks of rosin had once settled. It had been the very moment when a fertilized egg had latched onto her uterus. And so it was that during her first moments on this earth, her baby was exposed to the wonder and timeless beauty of music. And now, basking in the comfort that her life had been spared, Ivory, the infant who'd been granted the gift of life, performed a small somersault as she listened to the enchanting melody.

Guy sat in a cramped jail cell awaiting his pending arraignment. Following the arrest he'd waived legal counsel and had even refused a friend's offer to post bail. He was looking at one-to-ten years and a likely felony charge depending on how the judge chose to enforce the penal codes.

How ironic, he thought, that if a deranged gunman had shot Hanna, resulting in the death of their unborn child, the police report would have referred to their baby as a victim and the assailant would be sitting in jail on charges of murder. But instead, because their child's life was taken as a result of Hanna's own free will, their child was treated as though it had never existed, as if it were nothing more than a *choice*.

But the choice had not been his to make. And when, ultimately, he'd done everything in his power to save their child, he had been deemed a criminal, a crazed lunatic. And now, because Guy had refused to sit back and wait while his child's life was mercilessly exterminated, he was the one on trial. Not Hanna. And not the one who, despite having taken the Hippocratic Oath, had intentionally killed his baby.

Guy could hardly bear to think of his infant child's body lying somewhere in a landfill amidst garbage and other refuse, as if it were nothing more than trash. For his child there would be no funeral, no formal farewell, only the lamentable knowledge that a life which once was, was no longer.

Had she ever been counted among the living, her obituary might have read something like this:

Grey Evander, Conceived November 25th, 2010, Died April 1st, 2011 at 1:25PM--At the time of her death, she weighed nine ounces and was nearly six inches long. Grey was the daughter of Hanna Radcliff and Guy Evander of Santa Monica, CA. She is survived by her parents, as well as her maternal grandmother, Esther Radcliff, and paternal grandparents, William and Ruth Radcliff.

Some would say her conception was a mistake. Still others would say it was a gift. But to Grey, it was the joyful beginning to a sorrowfully short life which had been cut short at the hands of those who believed the right to choose did not belong to her.